Rhian Saadat is originally from south Wales, and lived in southern Spain, Cyprus and Dubai, before pausing in Paris in 1990 to buy a small restaurant, with her Persian husband, in the Marche aux Pûces at Clignancourt. Writing was to prove the antidote to this kind of existence, although she had already been writing children's fiction for Ginn, and in 1997 she joined the British Council writing workshop run by the American poet Alice Notley, and the late Douglas Oliver. During a brief return to the United Kingdom in 1998, Rhian completed the MA in creative writing at the University of East Anglia, before returning to Paris to organise this, her first collection of poetry. She also writes prose, and was a finalist in the 2002 Norwich Prize for short stories. She teaches at the International School of Paris.

Window Dressing for Hermès

Rhian Saadat

PARTHIAN

Parthian
The Old Surgery
Napier Street
Cardigan
SA43 1ED

www.parthianbooks.co.uk

First published in 2004
© Rhian Saadat 2004
All Rights Reserved

ISBN 1-902638-40-9
Editor: Richard Gwyn
Cover design by Marc Jennings
Printed and bound by Dinefwr Press, Llandybie, Wales

Typeset in Caslon 540 and GillSans by
type@lloydrobson.com

Parthian is an independent publisher which works
with the support of the Welsh Books Council and the
Arts Council of Wales.

British Library Cataloguing in Publication Data
A cataloguing record for this book is available from the
British Library.

For Anoush and Shahram

True Reality

Of this there is no academic proof in the world.
For it is hidden, and hidden, and hidden.
Rumi

Acknowledgements

The following poems have appeared previously in *Poetry Wales*: Fetishes at the Musée en Hèrbe, Bondage, Totemism in Papier Mâché, Writing a Love Song with a Stranger, For the Love of Dust, The Cartographer's Apprentice, Window Dressing for Hermès, Family Affair, Meeting with the Bulbophiles, Weavers, The Paris Mosque, Waiting for News, Offerings, Silk Route, Grey Raincoats, Culture Drift, Camel Deal, Hall of Mirrors, A Small Piece of Plumbing, Sequoia, Table of Orientation, Souvenirs from d'Urville, Saltalamcchia, Rowing a Gondola, Voyage of Discovery, Cumulonimbus, Being Lost – Stage 5, Cocoons from Orrefors.

El Mirador appeared in *The New Welsh Review*. Passing Through appeared in *Poetry London*. The Red Dress Incident appeared in *Reactions* anthology (2000). The Passion of Abbot Bienaimé, Larger then Life, and World's End appeared for the first time in the Parthian anthology *The Pterodactyl's Wing* (2003).

Contents

Window Dressing for Hermès

Hall of Mirrors

Passing Through

Window Dressing for Hermès

Fetishes at the Musée en Hèrbe

Who cares that you are developing your raku
technique in the piece that shows wild intercourse
between Bird Woman and the Crocodile? Or that
your passions veer towards Carrara marble, bronze
and steel, that you research your ideas in Etruscan art,
or the Mayan culture in Yucatan?
This is sexy stuff, and mustn't be disturbed by noises
off – academic mutterings over petits fours
smelling loudly of canned fish pretending to be
play-dough. We prefer the dangling skulls,

how the hair sprouts at sharp angles from the more
rounded bodily parts, the horns grafted where soft flesh
should be. These details are so moving we rush home
to make love before returning to complete the tour
of shamanic goats and wild cats, the fun-fur motorbike
with the naked girl dripping with embalming oil
and entitled, 'Study in Baked Clay'.

Bondage

There's something about the shape of boundaries,
linear, single-minded. Narrowly missing
                              the essence of things.

This is mutual attraction – a burning
for the unlocking of ideas, their bonne-bouches
rolling the tongue – and a risk of choking
on flavours so raw, our minds have no sounds
to contain them. They smoulder in the roof
of the mouth, grafting the settled skin
from its inverted nest of ridges where it hides
away the unborn cells of bleeding speech.
This is pain unfolding to remind us
that not everything new comes bright-sugared.

Described, this has the texture of barbed-wire,
of forks in the tongue, poking at a piece of flesh
torn clean from the body.
                    We have reached the crux of loving.

They cordon us off, so the crowd
        might watch us in safety.

Totemism in Papier Mâché

His work, unwritten, relies on Wax, and Gold;
two readings of a piece of art; A – lightweight,
clear. B – esoteric, a teasing discovery at the end
of some subtle digression. It's the Ethiopian way,
beginning with a coupling of obligatory dignitaries
decked out for celebratory war, their striped shields
matching their sunshine robes. Diptych, they can
be folded, face to face, and be carried away.
He'll do triptych too, but on commission.

Moving on, *Patriarch – Altarpiece – Termite Nest,
Megalith* and *Totem Pole* – colourful inventions
peopled by shiny and minute figures, matchstick arms
and dancing legs. His is relief work, in rainbow hues;
over here, a discourse on paper pulp, there, religious
recycling. These are tall stories – their beauty
being intransigence – and how they might all melt
away with the first drops of improbable rain.

Origami

A state of origami has been declared on the Côte d'Azur.
White gulls, the dimensions of cranes, are filling the sky,
like propaganda sheets from a rogue packet aeroplane
folding mid-air, first wing, then the balance, the beaks
so large that the tails must be yanked–so–to make them caw.
Ornithologists are concerned by the fifty-fold increase
between Monaco and Nice – almost broadsheet, noted one
and, as paper-birds go, surprisingly well synchronized.

Why couldn't we have had little boats, or Napoleonic hats?
pouted Madame from Villefranche. Just the other day
she lost her small dog, mid-stroll, when two sheets
of flapping cream descended on the creature, enveloped it
and took it out to sea – where they shredded it for pulp.
Residents have been advised to stay indoors, folding cats
from corrugated card.

Just a Suggestion

There are ways of doing this that needn't cause a ripple.
Remember drumming in the park, how you became the beat
and it became the vibrating skin of you? You tanned under
the light stroke of August drizzle, while the rest of us paled,
knowing it was a lifetime too late to get lessons.

And all I wanted, like I told you once before, was to place
my frozen summer hands between your rotating shoulder blades,
feel that thumping grow the length of my arms and back again,
all the pulsing of your body relayed into mine and ending, slap
bang, in the root of the brain.

And then for someone – and by that I mean just anyone –
to come up and place their cold-for-the-season finger-tips
on my scalp, and wait, for the rhythm, to rocket right through
the hair shafts, into the ears, down the length of their spine
and land in the toe-joints of their thermal stockinged feet.

And so on.

And then I thought, if you could carry on producing that heat,
these people might start to thaw, hook on to our gyrating bits,
using any small piece of themselves – wow – we might end up
with a stomping chain of the Northern translation of a rain
                                                    dance.

At some point, the sun would just have to come out.

Writing a Love Song with a Stranger

Let's avoid the jamming effect of conversation;
note, only, that I have washed my hair in chamomile,
grown it waist length in a week; that I have practised
humming in a mirror, that I can pirouette, right round
the other side of myself; that yesterday, I couldn't.

I'm tapping on the table, playing the full carafe d'eau,
refusing to pin a word on anything that can't be clapped to,
by spoons.

Let's keep the love song simple, deep, yet read as flat.
Rhythm's what's important – move the tables back.
Here we are – turning our madness into pas de deux –
when only yesterday, we wouldn't.

For the Love of Dust

'Beaux gisants, parlez-moi de la poussière des rêves...'
Louis Pons

I, too, have longings – hoards of them, hidden
in the dust along the shelves, graffitied by fingers
warmed in the premature sun as it probes
the gaps in the threadbare soul, waking the slow paths
of its wandering matter, eternally arriving, leaving,

unsettling. And now, you, with your long silences
like music, your breath another mist, sculpting shape
into the darkened cloud of me, flours and grains
blended to shrouds of grey and snippets of lost melody.
We stir an exodus – drift our weightless pieces through,
and beyond each other – land, silently.

I shake the dusters from the rooftops, your smile
a yawn. We dream in corners, rolling together
in clumped fogs of amnesia. Other lovers will come
to write their messages in us.

The Cartographer's Apprentice

Mapping was a skill she learned from birth,
ether tributaries leading into self, like leylines
running parallel with the rivers of milk,
purpled veins around nipples she would climb
with her mouth, her small feet grappling
against the uncharted air.

She discovered she could breathe it like water,
that it moved, moved her, moved clouds white
like milk curds across the unmarked sky
until they disappeared, leaving scuds of shadow
in her mirror eyes.

Her seamless skin was pleasing; its laced webs,
woven hairs, the pale green passages pulsing
out the eager hands. And the underside of flesh
where the sun cannot reach – so untrammelled
as to almost not exist, except as a membrane
between light and dark. Undulations
from her mother's voice wrote themselves
into the tiny cavities, inhaling, and exhaling
his new, undrawn world of sleep and plump flesh.

She grew herself into networks of line, curved
and curling – so that even her hair
grew in alluvial scribbles of red, leaving residual arcs
like haloes around her head.

And she draped herself with bolts of wool and wildest silks,
spiralling shells and images of a rambling sea,

stored them for the shapes they held – abyssal hills,
abyssal plains – secrets kept beneath a brim
of heaving O's and tangles, and hieroglyphic fish.

From her garde-robe of seaweed, she kept track
of the world, its roads leading nowhere, and those
leading back – painted them gold,
embroidered them in twine with tight-knotted end,
should they ever forget their beginnings.

L'Oeuf Sauvage

I'm trying to remember how I got here, egg on my face
and my shadow, its ovalness, growing longer by the minute.
I can hear your voices, distant and shouting, but first

                                impressions
are the musical ones – a slow, unfamiliar breathing syncopated

against a sharper thump; a gurgling in dark places. The higher
register of adrenalin. Raw, funky sounds and I can't help
but bop along a bit, emotionally stirred, frothed up and jiving
to arrangements like Blood in the Tunnels, Wind in the Gut.

But, am I chicken, goose or quail, and should it matter anyway,
now that I am resident, filling this air-pocket with my

                                  earthbound
angularities? I attempt a simple entrechat, and the walls beyond
my membranes flail, hum me a dance-image totally unique.
I begin to rotate my belly, my limbs. Body language, this, hot
with new beginnings.

The Red Dress Incident

C'était une robe étonnante!
is usually how the story begins,
yard after yard
of red silk
fanning its wings over a
neon-stripped world
like some exotic moth freed
from its forty-watt circus ring.

Mais, la belle?

Priceless, they assured the crowd.
Mlle Fonssagrives was firmly bound
to the top of the tower,
absolutely zero-risk involved
in the wearing of this piece.
A genuine Lelong meant
comprehensive insurance
paid for by Vogue.

Most of us, earthbound
in our low-voltage macs,
knew it was for real.

It was the way she fluttered out
into the sky, holding the rail
like an ice-cream cone – hey yup,
strawberry from Berthillon,
and a shade that matched the shoes.

When it happened – no,
she didn't fall, she didn't slip –
simply spiralled upwind,
leaving the crew in a flat spin about
dying film and exposed light,
so that no one got that one shot

of the naked creature in the fruity shoes
and red silk parachute.

Window Dressing for Hermès

'Madame Janet est une fée', concluded Cocteau. *'C'est l'artisanat du
miracle'*.
And truly, there is no stopping her, not since the resounding
success
of the 'Testament of Orpheus', during which we tried to
remember how
such scenecraft had nothing to do with selling lifestyle. It is
science,

Mesdames, Messieurs, an ignoring of the product to such a
degree,
it disappears from the viewing box entirely. Watch, as she brings
out
her shells and ribbons, her precious rocks bejewelled in gems of
plastic;
creates a statue crying blips of diamond superglue, startled white
feathers
for her dreadlocks.

Can you, passing by, spot those perfectly-crafted handbags?
Wafer-thin,
they are torn to rags, reassembled as an orgy of humming birds
spilling –
cornucopian – into a red leather brine. Velvet gloves are scented
flowers,
each palm cupped, swimming over with man-made-perfumed-
sunshine.

Madame Janet stands, spotlit in the centre, a mouthful of
shimmering pins,

staplegun wedged under one of her very up to the moment

lycra wings.

We wait for a miracle.

The Passion of Abbot Bienaimé

In his dreams, Abbot Bienaimé floats on clouds of honey.
He presents his ideas to the brothers – talks of God –
and a calling to explore the habits of bees.
'*Love*', he waxes, thinking in shades of nectar.

He denies them prayer, insists that matins
be devoted to the study of scent, and the hours
remaining spent in the gardens, with evensong
replaced by a silent Apiculture Hour.

Wood, willow, rush and clay, marble and glass
and even the humble canvas – all serve the abbot
in his unraveling. The bees will have none of his transparency,
and he is impatient for a glimpse of their sweet, interior life.

The brothers grow themselves a perfumed Eden, rosaries
of pollen. Bienaimé dissects the cloche hive, the Scottish hive,
The Debeauvoy, the Nutt, and his visions begin to heave
with strange mantra, a worldy sweat.

He considers Judgement, the golden skin of native girls
coming to him at night. They have wings and smell of acorns,
and they bind him in moss and trembling flowers. He lures them
with his ambitions, dandles them in his woven bowers.

In their dreams, the brothers pass through the gates of heaven.
They pray that the abbot might find the inner strength he seeks,
to fight the recurring madness, return them all to their gentle
                                                    cloisters,
return the crazed bees to their vacant oaks.

Migrating Bees

Egyptian bee-keepers resolved their pollination problems
with clay hives, stacked on rafts, set adrift to follow the Nile
as it wound itself beyond the farmsteads of Luxor.

In the mind's eye – a constant ring of honey, shade and taste
altering according to the crop grown on the reed-shielded
banks,
and the bees, pollen-drunk, velvet route-dancers.

Every Spring, Anderson and Tweedy shift a hundred
and sixty million bees between California and Minnesota;
The Cal-Minn Migratory Bees – on a bevy of flat-bed wagons.

Alfalfa one day, Cantaloupe the next – place-names exchanged
for the lay of the land and the heat of the midday diner,
the fumes from the highway blended with the scent of clover.

For six dollars, they will send you a queen, packed in a tight cell
of wood and plastic. Embalmed in such a manner, she can travel
intact,
navigating the whiteness of distance, the aerated taste of
bubble-wrap.

Family Affair

We'll be off then, as soon as we have the first signs.
And *en masse*, obviously; we could never go alone.
This journey requires orchestration of colour – synchronized
movement a million-fold – and a genetic memory held
as ingrained as any patterning of wings.

Orange and black, orange and black, we lay our ancient trail
and, escaping the North disguised as falling leaves,
we lock in to the smell of the sun.

As on any footpath, we take nothing
but a shared sense of *déjà vu*, handed down
            old to new,
                        old to new.
      Not one of us will make it there.
      It's not that kind of arrangement.
      We are symmetrically designed.
            Dying becomes an errand
                  we run for our young.

Meeting with the Bulbophiles

'A Menton, aux pieds de la falaise de la baie
de Garavan se niche au coin de Paradis'
Côte Sud 2002

They would plant themselves here, he said,
between the sea and those ancient olive trees,
and would propagate the kind of garden design
that rises, ruggedly, above the ground
before a final descent, thrusting up gold shoots

and jets of Spring water. Mottled heat and birdsong
were enveloped between ochre-walls and topiary,
the sea still loose on the other side, rattling pods
and small rhizomes up and down the beach,
blossoms falling in waves and tides

inventing kaleidoscopic mosaics. A note on the door
informed us they were Gone to Seed – back later.
We could hear their dog, barking at our scent –
imagined we could feel them, pushing through the floor,
the yellow plaster a slowly crumbling pot-pourri.

Hall of Mirrors

Weavers

I remember you as a weaver in Forqualquier,
the sign of the hand on the gate, at the end
of a long winding summer lane, and the small house

you had come to, years back, with a husband.
I remember him as a dervish, and thinking
what a sensible union yours must be – he

the weaver of movement, and you, the blender
of wools and silks; your creations – lucky charms
for the wearers. I bought a sunflower coat.

It's a little threadbare here and there, after all these years,
but I was anxious to wear it to visit you. To tell you
about the birds in my garden in Africa – describe

how the male weaves a nest of extraordinary skill,
and how the female inspects his handicraft
before confirming that she will mate with him.

The Paris Mosque

Here, the division between East and West
is simply defined by the choice of mint tea,
or milky coffee; the young artist in a corner

will include the fountain, the pool, the cat cleaning
itself under a sideboard of varnished baklava.
Like some miniature painting between pages,

we will appear as a host of similar people –
engrossed in our daily ablutions; the small print
in our Herald Tribunes, Figaros, Times

too small, even for decorative binding.
They will appear as towels, and we, unfolding them,
will be preparing ourselves, shyly, for bathing.

Waiting for News

I found your radio this morning
signalling from under the pillow,
its steady interference itching
my skin.

You've been wearing it all night
these last few years, locked
close to your cheek. It signals
to you on the hour – the news

from the East, prayers and songs
and arabesques escaping on waves –
urgent voices, shadowed black.
Their insistent intonations

link your blood to home, and to
somewhere beyond, the tiny room
holding your brother – silent, save
the signals he sends you, cell to cell.

Offerings

You always brought pomegranates
in your suitcases, not the small,
supermarket kind, but vast orange
baubles radiating a natural heat.
You encouraged us to eat savagely,
the pink of our mouths hitting the
combined juices of bulging seeds.
You would laugh at the impossibility

and how the English prefer pins.
Your excess baggage would ease
across the sitting room floor; carpets,
so densely knotted, they folded
into thin air; saffron hats
embroidered with poems,
strings of pistachio nuts.
An old telescope, a Persian astrolabe,
a Paradise garden on a miniature scale.

All this, and tales.
We wait for the latest one; time lost
in a Tehran jail. *I was head gardener*
you smile, fainter now.
I grew pomegranates, gathered dates.

Cutting the flesh from another fruit,
your shirt-sleeves rolled.
We read the scars,
begin to understand why your hands
tremble
without something to hold.

Shaykh Abdullah

When I have had such men before my camera
my whole soul has endeavoured to do its duty
towards them in recording faithfully the greatness
of the inner as well as the features of the inner man.
                    Julia Margaret Cameron

Imagine a lifetime spent seeking the source
of some river; and the life is not yours, but another
disguised in such ways that cancel you out –
a camouflage, in shades of secrecy and alluvia,
a pseudonym suggesting something more indigenous.

Mrs. Cameron's photographic study reveals nothing
of your travels. You are elsewhere, and your alter ego
appears to be staring at lakes, somewhere beyond
the composition. You will be exhibited in Bond Street
as an exotic object; at Colnaghi's, as a British spy.

Somewhere, in the divide, the spring that eluded you.

Silk Route

There is always a deeper layer, hidden.

We have come to find the savants, the stars
in our eyes, and they tell us they have gone,
long buried by the conquerors, discoverers
of a different time. We leave without paying

still looking for the crossroads, the silk route
leading to the transparent mountains
where the people are made from a clay so fine
they remain invisible unless held, turning
into the sun. We appreciate this feeling.
It is for this we have come.

Instead, a modern city greets us, grinning
through the night. Where are the minarets?
Distant voices are urging us to worship.
It's a western tune, with an oriental beat.
We kneel, dig holes in the ground for dead phrases.

We will leave them there, move on with the shadows
ahead of morning, still seeking the land of porcelain.

The Water Carrier

The Kurdish woman is wearing her best dress
for collecting the water. It is a vivid blue garment,
embroidered in silver moons and mirrors,
chinking together lightly
as she lifts her skirts to step across the stones
bridging Qalat Dizah.

The dress is her only one, and around her neck she wears
a gold chain with a garnet at the centre the size
of a child's small, clenched fist, and her dark hair
is held back in a brightly patterned, gauzy scarf. Nationless,
this woman can wear anything, and so she chooses
to be conspicuous in a vast, bleached space.

When the water is finished, her husband will use the bucket
To carry mortar shells to the top of the hill.
The other men wait for him there, dug in close
to the heart of the land – guarding the borders of their
                                                    existence,
watching for the bright dress crossing the sand.

Grey Raincoats

There I am, and again, here. In the background,
the famous gardens of Barg-i-Fin. Each of my in-laws
is dressed in similar fashion, recognisable only
by our headscarves. Mine came from Agnes B, Paris,
theirs were from Chanel of Tehran. Our shapeless coats
are indistinguishable, loose. And that's heat, rising.

Mariam does not care for any external frivolity.
She's the one in black, head to foot, but her smile
is still the most convincing. Madia, younger, wears
a generous helping of make-up, and, beneath the coat –
a mini-skirt and minier t-shirt, *I Love America!*
stretched between her breasts.

Mariam had been explaining about the Ayatollah *Dot.Com*.
He is modern, and young Iranians appear to like him.
Madia snorts. She has just opened her own health club
in the centre of town; sunbeds, beauty, mixed-sex hammam.
Her sunglasses glint on the top of her head. For her,
revolution can't come fast enough.

Friday, they announced, we would visit the Bag-i-Dilgusha –
Garden of Heart's Ease. Madia winks. She was planning
to wear nothing, under her plain grey coat. That's me,
there, looking wilted. Madia is the one in the orange scarf
just slipping away from her forehead, a spiral of wild
bottle-blonde hair escaping from beneath.

El Mirador

From excavated pollen samples we know
now that the garden was originally planted
with almond trees; that the central fountains
were certainly surrounded by vast tulip beds,
that there wasn't a patch of earth left naked.

Dense orange blossom would have canopied
the courtyard, giving play to the shadow pairs
you imagined you could see; and the perfume
created by humid longings came from petals.
Rumour has it your fate was watching others

making love. We have no evidence of this –
simply – that the garden surrounded the tower,
that it was breathtaking, out of this world, and that
the fortress was made so hastily, magic power
must have held it from crumbling.

You must have perished like bees, fumbling
between glass and honey.

Culture Drift

Before we start on the gardens, and after
we jump through the fire, we must collect
sloughed bark from the forest floor.
The others are choosing flat pieces, and some,
slightly hollow. I prefer the pieces that curl
away from the tree in ringlets, resembling
ancient documents, dropped, mid-proclamation.

For this New Year, then, we are to compete
with the Great Gardens, attempting to replicate them,
perfectly, and in miniature. Our host, Reza, chooses
the Bagh-i-bulbul – Shah Abbas's Garden
of the Nightingale. His wife wants to assemble
its pavilion of Eight Paradises. He tells her
this is cheating.

Other guests settle for Gardens of the Vineyard,
of the Mulberries, the Throne. I am left dithering
in a European fog. Vignanello perhaps, or Barbirey?
Grandmother and her chapel crowd surface, suddenly,
and a bus trip to Bodnant. The heat, and the flowers,
conjure her compact powder, boiled sweets.
But it was later in the year – a summer perhaps.

Standing knee-deep in the river, we hold our creations
above the water, launch them, one by one, and watch
as they disappear with the current, each one a ship,
garlanded for Spring. My garden is curled at the edges
so that it spins like a dinner plate, returning to me, again
and again. One last push, and it finds the water's meaning,
tumbles away, at last, downstream.

Camel Deal

Tails, we lost, they kept the jeep, the maps;
we took the camels anyway,
rode into the sunset keeping, best we could
for first-timers, the galloping in time
to the women's drums. It would never do
to appear as amateurs, lost in sand
and strange rhythms.

Our ululations were as good as any
ever heard this side of east; a ten second blast
could ripple a sand dune at ten paces,
and the beasts, we imagined, could be trained
to speak our languages, or at very least
to respond to simple proddings.

But the sun sank, and we, still riding on, passing
caravanserai, oases, dunes unsung and laughing
at the sight of us, nodding to sleep in the low arc
of our camel skins, their humps vacated, freed
to juggle again to that self-made beat, our feet
at odds with the balance, soles braced against
the freezing drone of the night.

Hall of Mirrors

We would all prefer our lions to lie on fine large rugs;
this is the anteroom, and as far as any visitor may enter.
Please, be at ease – enjoy the elephants, the royal gazelles,
and the rhinoceros can be yours for the evening. We dine

later, when there is so much more to uncover. Your business
is mapped in the heavens; we can smell it too, in your vodka.
Nothing is ever as it seems, and your ambassador's kind gift
of a chandelier doesn't fool us for one minute. Take a peek,

if you will, although our women are still in their quarters,
oiling their hair and brown bodies. Those secret rooms
have powers to multiply caresses – we can watch ourselves –
visit infinity. You, of course, will not participate. Our home

is yours, but only as far as this doorstop. Solid gold,
and welcoming.

Alchemy

They worked, not as artists, but as alchemists
    of Scarpa and Venini – glassmakers

They created their blueprints from colours,
viewed every gradation of opaqueness
against warm waters, cold water, aqua pazza,
low tides and high winds, considered technique
to be brought into play; variegato

with illusory gold-leaf for shelter, transparent
towers for keeping the sky at bay; inciso
for reflections before sunrise, for shadows
beneath bridges, in doorways, each blown
from a single ball of that nameless shade
beyond the obsidian rendez-vous; sommaro

for the planets of light caught after cooling,
fusing fate with chandeliers of flossed ice,
spun salt with opalescent moonfish
and stargazers with somnambulists; tessuto

for the invisible pathways between those
who never meet, but sense the proximity
of parallels.

Cocoons from Orrefors

On a toujours besoin d'un cocon chez soi...
                                                    Crevoisier

His shadow is longer at the end of the day
than it is at the beginning.

That comes from spinning an existence,
when he should be blowing tumblers
for a living.

Instead, he works a ballet with his stream
of thin glass veins, winding them
with a transparent gaze around each blown soul
of his obsession. He doesn't try to make
the ends meet, and there are holes
where the rain comes in and the light, escaping
back into itself, glimmers in returning.

You get the feel of these things, after a while,
caught between earth and water, imagine
a time when you were folded inside,
on the brink of emerging. Strange though,
how this idea begins to bend, rolls itself
slowly into certain remembering.

A Small Piece of Plumbing

You won't find any U-bends here.

They have used the finest materials,
key-holed and threaded, mapped
diversions just under the skin, leaving
underground pathways coiled
for growing. He will grow, after all.
'But perhaps not the same as other kids.'
They prepared us from the beginning.
Note landmark developments – speech.
We shall have to wait and see. *From here,
there's just no way of telling.*

From here, there's no way of telling.

You can't see the neatly-placed tubing,
a sigh of a line, from behind the skull,
a straight slip down the chest,
into the guts. There's a pump for shunting,
an invisible package in the back of the head.

In the back of the head there's a crescent
moon of stitching. We search by the light
of it for ways back into ourselves, through
the sealed bones of our fontanelles –
my husband with his slaughtered sheep,
bled at the throat, fed to the less-fortunates.
I read books – *Your Developing Child* – stare
at spaces between the words, willing each one
to leak some clue. My hair is falling out
in large phrases, into a sea of no telling.

Sequoia

Double-trunk sequoia are the best
for building tree-shacks; you enter
head first, through the driftwood
floor, pulling yourself up on the elbows.

Some, coming here to visit, compare it
to being born again. Standing upright,
they say they can't wait for the wind
to begin blowing us, side to side. Usually

they take their leave before it happens.
I've decided it's the noises they must like,
the silence of a world made from nothing
that wasn't here already, the sigh of a wing,

the tree growing steadily around, higher now
than the hut itself, and singing its ancient lullaby.
They never mention the feathers, though –
owl feathers spread evenly over the floor.

Just as well. Imagine explaining the crowd
that gathers here every stormy night – me,
and my ancestors; we go as far back as the day
this tree took root, thrust its head skyward.

Table of Orientation

I have designed it as a temple, in three parts;
all that happened before birth, now, and eternity.
You are here, like me, just about in the middle.

I deliberately placed it under the old lime tree
so that travellers would know where to find it,
eat their sandwiches in peaceful surroundings
unaware that the remains of a murdered hermit
lie in clingfilm in the local Mairie; that the kink
in the trunk, half way up, is not some quirkiness
of nature.

We can see for miles, standing here, identify
every mountain range, locate the orchid fields,
dwell on the beauty of existence. Wanderers
have passed this way for hundreds of years,
stopping at the tree, locating where they were,
where it was they wanted to be.

Passing Through

Passing Through

In this country, wood is scarce. People are poor,
but welcoming. A great thick door like this
is an emblem of wealth, the opening of which
might take forever since the transverse beams
must first be carefully dismantled. All this time

your host speaks no word,
and the only sounds are from the slow careful
drawing of the bolts, and his inhaling, exhaling
you consider like some mnemonic greeting.

The frame around the door is an heirloom; see
the carvings – the growth of a world clinging
to its own roots – you can do that sort of thing
here – it's decorative, explaining the traditions
of those you meet. It's the only reasoning you
will encounter. And the small window? Yes,
they like to look out, take a peep at those
who come knocking. Nowadays, it doesn't
happen very often. Listen to that creak
of an opening. A thin stream of daylight

on daylight, and his beckoning hand. You step
in, and out again – straight through and into
open country. You note his balanced sense
of out and in, without the necessary trappings.

He is smiling now, inviting you to sit with him,
take tea from a samovar, steaming away
in the grass. But first, he locks the door again,

peers through the opening, smoothes the wood.
Adds another leaf to the carving.

Souvenirs from the Voyages of d'Urville and Dumoulin

Apart from the headdress with the black and white feathers,
there will be an atlas with fifty-two, never-before-seen, maps
of the other side of the planet. And there will be a dugout's prow
from the Solomon Isles – a head with wide-open eyes, guarding
sailors against the sea's bad spirits.

La Terre Promise, the explorers called it, coming home, emptying
Astrolabe and *Zelée* of their treasures – pumice stone people
from the Admiralty Isles, fish hooks from the Society Isles,
spears,
axes, *ethnic* bones, and a club of the Marquesas' *u'u* tribe,
with a remarkable patina of wear and tear, and passing time

and a collection of many curious dolls, from the Hopi and the
Zuni
of New Mexico – each one carved from a single root of the Aspen
tree
and painted colours accorded to the compass points – black for
the zenith,
the nadir – grey, with the final addition of amulets and – again
– feathers
giving Dumoulin's bulging corvettes an aspect of their own
plumage,

as they settle themselves upon the cool, familiar rim of the
world. The dolls
will later be prized by exiles, charmed by their childlike patterns
– consumed
by their unfaded expressions of startled loss.

Saltalamacchia

Will you take your elephant *with* the baldachin,
or without? Stirred from its long sleep,
the creature will carry you far, night and day,
if you order the optional accessories.

Perhaps you wish to travel further, in which case
could you not be tempted with a school of fish,
assorted sizes fired for a crackled glaze, flicked
tails, and dinner plate eyes, even for the gaze
of the minnows?

Where is it exactly you wish to go, and when?
We have a wonderful design for a cockerel, here,
crowing on and on, so that you never sleep.
If you're kind to him, he'll keep you awake
long enough to circle the world, and back again.

All your disused dreams may be stored here,
for no extra cost, in a very simple, lidded bowl.

Rowing a Gondola

was just a very small part of the business.
We should, perhaps, have chosen elephants,
their hides our folded itineraries of beaten paths,
their perfectly lolloping symmetry rocking us aloft
in boat-shaped jangling palankeen.

But, we might have missed the smell of the sea –
the wind from the high domed sky blowing slantwise
through our dampened features, skin salted like the fish
that would take us through the winter stretch, stored
nose-high in the felze, where the cushions used to be.

It was the beckoning of the open space, never the clicking
latch that urged us on to islands bathing in waters,
where the wake from our craft lapped at geraniums
and sleeping eels curled on dusty window-sills, their shadows
as long as the blown glass poles we used to steer our way

between the isthmus of refracted light – in which glass
became air, and the cooling air – a shimmering reminder
of the need to keep moving in our own sliding mirage.

Voyage of Discovery

It is so easy, this road, that it may be travelled sleeping
                                        Mir Yahya Kashi

There it was, our holiday craft, propped up on stilts
in the shallows of the lagoon, lilting into the afternoon
sun, its mainsail beckoning us to hurry,

as if its departure was imminent.

The soft creak and murmur of timber was soporific,
and, stowing fruit, we slept, slept off the side-effects
of living, slept a steady drumming of cloth against
the spar. When we stirred, we could see in all directions,
and our vessel was surrounded by water. It was a whale

of poon wood and coconut rope, sealed with oil and sugar.

The days and nights lost track of us; we took our bearings
with orange peel eased from the flesh in perfect spirals, held
in the palm, thrown to the foam. Our observations
revealed we were nearing the curled out edges
of some magnificent adventure – we would dream it,

an ocean, littered with horizons. Waxed coracles closing
into perfect spheres, opening out again. Riding the crest

wave after wave after wave.

B-15

The satellite image recorded the cracks for nine years
before this happening, beamed them back to Earth. Ice –
a slice the size of Delaware, snapped free

turned slowly into the currents and the banshee winds.
We give her a smaller, temporary tag; to name too carefully

is to form attachment, a feeling for a land that wants none of us.

Beneath the numb bulk, a garden spawned by Paradise,
transparent, raw, littered with new beginnings, pearls
worn deep under lace skirts and coldest skin.

The berg moves west, and the air around her shimmers.
She will calve herself soon, and into smaller selves, each one of
                                                                                    her
believing in larger seasons, in her own boundless sense of
                                                                    immortality.

Larger than Life

One degree of latitude for each dream of the Tropics.
The arrival of light, and we alter course – chuck dates
at the trilling of the Weddell seals. These are Julian Days,
and through them we can peek at pleats of buzzing frazzle-ice
shot with chaotic pattern. Sundogs howl their crystal rainbows
and seawater spouts, sky high.

Larger than life, they warned us. Try to slip past the jellyfish.
But there she looms – in a space shaped from imagining –
metabolism spun across snowmelted time – the sea her air,
the ceiling of ice her planet, and us, orbiting in the wake
of her waltzing drift. She is every colour yet to be created,

flounced organza membranes, ripple-silk lips, and a filigree trail
of substance more akin to memories, before birth, of a journey
that begins in being here – seeing this – understanding only
how we are the shadows, bead-black, and she, the myth.

Cumulonimbus

The gales swept in from the channel this week,
forced them to close *le parc*, and our shutters –
old hinged-metal things – irritated night, nagged it
towards the frayed edge of morning. The washing line

snapped, streaking up beyond the flattened trees
as if twenty sodden towels were nothing more,
or less, than silken prayer flags, stringing their way
to good fortune. Candy-striped and tartan,

they were flapping around for absent mountains
and unnamed masses of snow-packed stone.
There is a ritual to climbing. Tinkering like surgeons
over mounds of felled wood, we tap in the first piton,
disappear one by one, through fleeting low cloud.

Being Lost – Stage 5

I have never really missed that feeling of the ground
beneath my feet; halfway, and the scree provides
as good a place as any for sleep. And from here

I can just make out the land far below, one blue vein
of river and the quarry, a small red stain spilling over,
sliding out of focus. Volcanic now, I always imagined

it an indentation, on the borders of knowing home,
and flight. My porta-ledge sways through ninety degrees
and I fold my new clothes into neatly settled piles,

smooth the rolled tunnel of chrysalis silk.

Five thousand feet and swinging, base camp
is a shanty town of pulleys and rope, a vertical slant
against which the wind cracks and bounces its confusion.

Edgeless existence, and it isn't even cold. Tomorrow,
if the weather holds, I think I could reach the summit.

World's End

Yabrai Yanchang, last village before the desert,
and the lake is the garnet of halophyte. The land is quartz,
its reach so high, you'd be right to mistake it for mountains.
Each dune piles itself over another, creating tombs
for the ancestors' hills – their ripples buried echoes
of their own haunted past. The old woman, Diudiu,
sees the ghost each evening. They rise from the fire
as she sits with the goats.

The new year is designated Year of the Mountain;
Diudiu knows nothing of this. In her recurring dreams
there are visions of a distant city. It is flat and shiny
and she would be forced to leave her flock behind.
Wind blows to settle in her shelter. In the Spring
she will sweep it back, remind the spirits of strange birds
she has seen, flying far beyond the flat calm of the lake.